Bear Grylls

This survival skills handbook has been specially put together to help young adventurers just like you to stay safe in the wild. Standing at the peak of a towering mountain, looking out at the world below, is a phenomenal experience, and there are mountains on every continent, so you'll never run out of new peaks to explore. This book will teach you what clothes and equipment to bring, and how to keep yourself safe as you explore the top of the world.

Bear.

CONTENTS

WHAT IS A MOUNTAIN?

All over the world, on every single continent, you will find areas of ground that are higher than the rest of the surrounding area – hills and mountains. Not only are mountains a lot of fun to explore, but they can also be useful for survival.

Hills and mountains

The difference between a hill and a mountian isn't always clear, and can vary depending on where you are. In the UK and Ireland, a mountain is any summit over 610 m above sea level. The Great Soviet Encyclopedia, on the other hand, says any mountain below 200 m is a hill. Mountains are generally considered taller and steeper than hills, but in Scotland all mountains are often called hills, no matter what their height!

BEAR SAYS

Humans have always used hills and mountains to help them look out for invaders, find food, and provide safe places to live.

Major mountain ranges

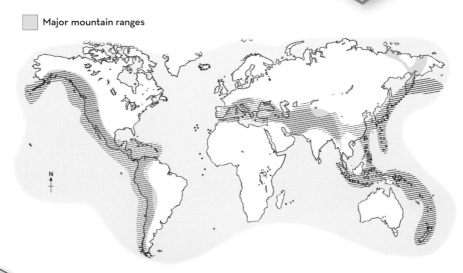

Record-breaking mountains

Ben Nevis, Scotland – 1,345 m
Tallest mountain in the UK

Mount Everest, Himalayas – 8850 m
Highest mountain in the world

K2, Himalayas – 8612 m
Second highest mountain in the world

Kilimanjaro, Tanzania– 5895 m
Tallest mountain in Africa

Mauna Kea, Hawaii – over 10,000 m
(4,207 m above sea level)
Tallest mountain in the world (though
over half is underwater)

Denali, Alaska, US – 6194 m
Tallest mountain in North America

MOUNTAIN FEATURES

Mountains are much more than just big hills. Every mountain is a unique collection of many different features. It's very important to know all the names and types of mountain features, so you will understand any maps or signs you might need to follow.

Dune – A loose hill made of sand, formed by wind or flowing water.

Crag – A mountain formed by a glacier passing through and eroding softer material, leaving behind harder rock.

Pingo – A mound of ice, covered with earth, found in the Arctic and Antarctic.

Scree slopes – A collection of small rock fragments that have gathered at the bottom of a mountain, caused by rockfall from above.

Talus slopes – A collection of broken rock fragments, usually larger than a man's fist.

Snow slopes – Some mountains are snow-covered for the entire year, but in other areas it melts in the summer.

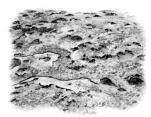

Hard ground – Rocky soil that has been firmly compacted and will not give way under your weight.

Grassy slopes – Not usually a continuous field, these may contain thick patches of growth.

Thick brush – this can be difficult to pass through, so take another route if possible.

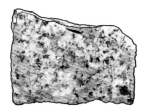

Igneous rock (e.g. granite, basalt) – formed by volcanic magma cooling.

Sedimentary rock (e.g. sandstone, chalk) – formed by sediments being compressed on the bottom of the ocean.

Metamorphic rock (e.g. slate, marble) – formed by extreme pressure and/or heat.

VOLCANOES

There are three basic types of mountain: volcanic, fold, and block mountains. Volcanoes are formed when a tectonic plate gets pushed below another, and melted rock (magma) from below the Earth's crust is forced into the air, becoming lava. When the lava cools, it builds up into a volcanic mountain.

Dormant volcano

It can be difficult to tell the difference between a volcano that is dormant (sleeping), and one that is extinct, and will never erupt again. Generally, if there are no written records about a volcano erupting, it is considered extinct.

Mount Vesuvius

Mount Vesuvius is considered one of the most dangerous volcanoes in the world. It is near Naples, in Italy, and is most famous for its eruption in 79 AD, which destroyed the town of Pompeii, killing over 1,000 people.

Fourpeaked Mountain

Fourpeaked Mountain in Alaska, US, was thought to be extinct until it suddenly erupted in 2006. The last eruption before this was 10,000 years ago, in 8000 BCE!

BEAR SAYS

Always assume a volcano could erupt. Some can be dormant for many hundreds of thousands of years, but climate change may trigger an eruption.

HOW TO SURVIVE A VOLCANO ERUPTION

Volcanic eruptions can be extremely sudden, dramatic, and scary, or hardly noticeable. Luckily, most volcanoes are carefully monitored by scientists, so warnings can usually be given before there is an event. Volcanoes can be unpredictable, though, so it's important to know how to respond to an unexpected eruption.

Volcano survival tips

- Be aware of the warning systems in place for the local area.
- If you hear a warning siren, turn on the radio to listen for instructions.
- Have a planned escape route. Some regions produce maps showing probable paths of lava flow. Be aware of these and work out how long it will take to escape the area. Plan more than one route.
- Make sure everyone knows the escape plan.
- Have a bag with food and equipment ready so you can leave quickly if necessary.
- Wear long sleeves and trousers.
- Keep hydrated and carry plenty of water.
- If you aren't told to evacuate, stay indoors with all the doors and windows closed until you are told it is safe to come out.
- If you can't get to shelter, go to higher ground.
- Protect yourself from pyroclastics (flying rocks and debris) by crouching on the ground and covering your head with your arms, backpack, or anything else to hand.
- There might be poisonous gases. Wear goggles, a mask, a respirator, or a wet piece of cloth over your mouth and nose if possible.
- Never try to cross a lava flow.
- Stay away from areas where ash is falling.

listen to the radio for instructions to evacuate or find shelter

crouch on the ground and cover your head to protect yourself from pyroclastics

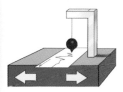

a seismometer can measure volcanic activity

FOLD MOUNTAINS

Some of the biggest and most well-known mountain ranges are fold mountains, including the Himalayas, the Rockies, the Andes, and the Alps. These ranges are formed where tectonic plates meet, and include some of the biggest mountains in the world.

How are fold mountains formed?

The Earth's crust, or lithosphere, is made up of separate plates, called tectonic plates, which move around independently of each other. Normally, the movement is so gradual that we can't feel it, but sometimes two plates will crash together, causing an earthquake. When two plates collide like this, rocks crumple and fold upwards, forming mountains.

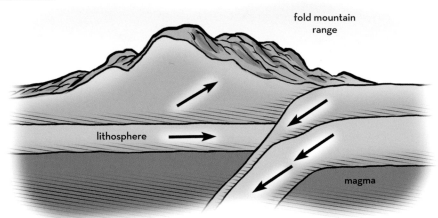

fold mountain range

lithosphere

magma

Ancient seabeds

Sedimentary rock is formed on the sea floor, before being pushed up to form mountains. For a long time, this idea of how mountain ranges are formed was just a theory, but mountaineers found fossils of ancient sea creatures high up on mountains, proving it right. In fact, you can find fossilized sea life on the top of Mount Everest!

FAULT-BLOCK MOUNTAINS

Fault-block mountains are created when two plates move past each other at a fault (gap) in the Earth's crust. If the rocks are higher on one side than the other, mountains and valleys are formed. The blocks created can be hundreds of kilometres long. The high areas are called "horsts", and the low valleys are called "grabens".

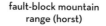

fault-block mountain range (horst)

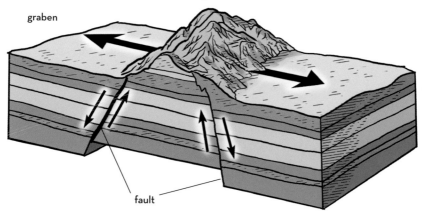

graben

fault

BEAR SAYS

The Great Rift Valley in East Africa and Death Valley in California, US, were formed in this way.

MOUNTAIN WEATHER

Mountains are so big that they can affect the weather dramatically. The weather can change rapidly in mountains, and the weather at the foot and the summit can be vastly different. It is important to understand these changes when exploring a mountain, so that you can make sure you have the correct clothing and equipment.

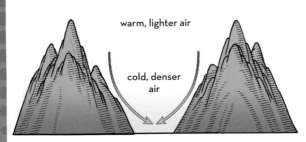

warm, lighter air

cold, denser air

Temperature inversion

It is usually safe to assume it will get colder as you climb a mountain. Occasionally, though, there is the opposite effect, called a temperature inversion. Cold air gets trapped and forms clouds at low levels, while it is warmer and sunny higher up.

Effects on rainfall

Mountains have a huge effect on rainfall. Moist air moving over a mountain is forced upwards, the temperature of it quickly drops, and clouds and rain are created. If it is already raining, the rain gets heavier. Over the peak of the mountain the air moves downwards and becomes much drier. One side of a mountain range is often much drier than the other side due to this effect, called a rainshadow. It is helpful to know which side of a mountain will be wetter when exploring, so you can make a decision about where to build a shelter in the case of bad weather.

area of rainshadow

warm, moist air

dry air

Wind

Many useful survival skills rely on wind conditions. Sometimes you need to make sure the wind is blowing away from you, and sometimes it needs to be blowing towards you, depending on what you need to do. Knowing different terms will help, too – if you get your leeward and windward or your upwind and downwind mixed up, your safety might be at risk.

Windward and leeward

The side of a mountain where it is wetter and windier is called the "windward" side, while the drier side is known as the "leeward" side.

windward   leeward

BEAR SAYS

If you are tracking an animal, stay downwind of it. This way, the wind is blowing your scent away from the animal, and it won't be able to smell you.

Prevailing winds

The prevailing wind is the direction where the wind most commonly blows in a certain area. Knowing the prevailing wind will help you to plan your route and shelter.

Upwind and downwind

If you are moving in the same direction as the wind, with the wind at your back, you're moving downwind. If you're moving against the wind, you are upwind.

Lighting a fire

If you're lighting a fire in windy conditions, you don't want to risk flames spreading to your shelter and equipment. Make sure you build your shelter downwind of the fire. This will also prevent smoke blowing in your face.

EQUIPMENT

There are many different climates on mountains, you will need different equipment depending on the conditions, or even a range of equipment. It is best to ask someone experienced in mountain exploration what you will need to bring.

avalanche transceiver

rucksack

camera

compass

crampons

carabiners

climbing harness

flint and steel

duct tape

first aid kit

tent

14

food

portable GPS

headtorch

sun hat

climbing axe

rope

flask

map

matches

suncream

knife

mobile phone

sleeping bag

shovel

emergency blanket

sleeping mat

water

walking sticks

CLOTHING

Your clothing should be dependent upon the weather and conditions on the particular mountain you are visiting. A day trek up a small local hill will require nothing particularly special, but a week up a high, cold mountain will mean that a very different and more extensive set of clothing will need to be carefully selected.

fleece jacket or vest

bandana or buff

BEAR SAYS

Working properly, your body is like a furnace that generates heat. In cold weather, we need to preserve our body heat with appropriate clothing.

gloves or mittens

insulating hat

waterproof trousers

goggles

insulating jacket

rain jacket with hood

socks, plus spares

sun hat

walking boots

snow shoes

base layers

gaiters

fleece trousers

climbing
shoes

RIVERS AND STREAMS

A stream starts with melting snow or rainwater collecting at the highest point in the area and flowing downhill, usually towards the sea, gaining water from other sources along the way. We need fresh water to survive, so it is important to know where to find drinking water on a mountain.

BEAR SAYS

People often live close to water, so if you are lost it is a good idea to find water and follow it downhill until you reach civilization.

How to cross flowing water

- Before you cross, consider the following: depth, temperature, entry and exit points, speed of the water, and the capability of your group members.
- If alone, use a strong pole to support you. Always keep at least one leg and the pole, or both legs, on the bottom. Cross diagonally downstream.
- Look ahead and shuffle your feet forwards, feeling for the bottom as you go.
- If you are with others, put your arms around each other's back and hold onto their clothing at the waist.
- Put the strongest person upstream and cross with them slightly ahead of everyone else.
- If you are in a group of three, join together facing inwards with the heaviest person facing the water flow. Then take turns to take a step.
- If you are swept off your feet, keep your feet together and point them downstream. Don't try to stand up until you are in calm water.

Types of waterway

waterfall

BEAR SAYS

Never cross any water that is deeper than the groin level of the shortest member of the group unless your survival depends upon it.

glacier

river

pool

mouth

spring

stream

ASCENDING AND DESCENDING

Climbing routes are given grades that describe the difficulty and danger of the route. These grading systems vary, so make sure you are using the correct information. Knowing what grade a mountain is will help you plan your expedition – you don't want to end up on a challenging mountain without preparing properly beforehand.

Getting downhill

Once you have got to the top of the mountain, admired the view, and rested, the next step is to get back down again safely. Too many accidents have occurred because people don't take care, rush, or are tired on the way down. Make sure you allow plenty of time, plan properly, and use a technique appropriate to the type of terrain.

BEAR SAYS

Don't get complacent – descending is as dangerous as ascending a mountain, so you need to be just as careful on the way down.

Walking off

This is usually the best way to descend if at all possible, as it is simple – you just walk! Be aware you might end up scrambling down gullies and bashing your way through bushes. Make sure you know your route and stick to it. Watch your footing, too – when walking down a steep slope it is easy to pick up speed, which can lead to slips and falls.

Downclimbing

If the route is steep, you may need a safety rope. Always go for the safest option. If you don't feel confident, don't do it and don't let other people persuade you to climb down if you aren't comfortable. Usually the most experienced climber should go first.

Rappelling

This is simply making a controlled slide down a rope. Usually used to get off cliff tops safely, this is something that needs to be taught by an expert using specialized equipment that is checked every time it is used.

Lowering

Lowering is when one person lowers another down a cliff with a climbing rope. It is quick and easy, but can easily go wrong with a silly mistake. Always make sure the rope is long enough and tie a stopper knot (there are several types) on the free end. Again, this should only be attempted under the guidance of a qualified person.

✗ BEAR SAYS

A strong knowledge of knots is a huge help if you want to climb safely.

how to tie a stopper knot

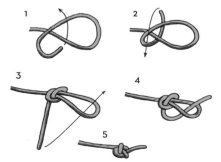

1
2
3
4
5

MOUNTAIN SPORTS

Mountain climbing is a lot of fun, but there is so much more you can do on a mountain. There is a huge variety of different fun sports and activities you can do – whether you like climbing, skiing, or even hangliding, there's something for everyone!

Rock climbing

In this sport, people climb up, down, and across natural rocks. It's a lot of fun, and is a fantastic workout for your entire body! There are competitions where people will race across the rocks, trying to complete the course first, without falling.

BEAR SAYS

Always make sure you have permission to do your sport in the area and stick to agreed routes and places.

Aid climbing

The most popular type of climbing, this is done with the aid of ropes and other safety equipment. This is great for beginners, as the ropes provide support and stop you from falling.

Free climbing

This is done under the climber's own strength without the support of ropes. Equipment is sometimes used, but only for protection rather than support.

Bouldering

This is climbing across short, low routes without any equipment for support. You need to have a lot of strength to try bouldering!

Skiing
Skiing is not just a sport – it can also be a useful way of travelling around on snow. Originally done on wooden skis, people have been skiing for thousands of years.

Alpine skiing
In this exhilarating sport, the toe and heel of your boot is attached to the ski. Ski or chair lifts carry you to the top of the slope so you can whizz down!

Snowboarding
Similar to skiing, in snowboarding both of your feet are attached to one board. Many people find snowboarding easier to pick up than skiing.

Mountain biking
This involves riding specially-designed bikes off road. It's important to watch out for other people using the area, and make sure you have permission to cycle in the area.

Fell running
Similar to cross-country running or orienteering, this involves running up and down hills or mountains. Sometimes you will need to navigate a route as you run.

Hang gliding
In this extreme sport, you are launched off a hill, attached to a giant, stringless kite called a hang glider. It is kept in the air with the help of warm air rising in columns called "thermals".

MOUNTAIN SHELTERS

If you are planning to spend the night on a mountain, a tent is often the easiest option. There are a huge variety of lightweight tents that are easy to carry. If you have to spend an unplanned night on the mountain, there are many other options for finding and building shelter – you just need to know where to look!

Finding a place to build your shelter

Location is everything when it comes to building a shelter. Choose a suitable site on the drier, more sheltered side of the mountain. Make sure your shelter is safely away from loose rocks that could fall, and steer clear of areas like ditches that might flood if it rains.

Mountain huts

These huts, high up on mountains, can be found in many countries, so it is useful to do your research before you travel. They range from small, basic shelters to fully-staffed hostels, and are a great option if you have to spend an unplanned night on a mountain.

Bivvy bags

This very simple shelter is basically an orange plastic bag, big enough for one person, which will keep you sheltered from the elements in an emergency. They may not be the most comfortable shelter, but they're cheap, easy to carry, and could save your life in an emergency.

Hooped bivvy bags

These are more expensive than a basic bivvy bag, but slightly more comfortable. They are basically a small tent big enough for a person but not any kit. Considering how light many tents are nowadays, a tent may be a better option than a hooped bivvy bag, as they will keep your equipment dry, too.

Natural shelters

If you are short of time and equipment, natural shelters are often easy to find on a mountain. A rock shelter is a shallow cave at the base of a cliff, often under waterfalls. Always check for sleeping animals before you make shelter – you don't want to disturb any wildlife in its natural home! Rocks will capture the sun's heat in the day and radiate it back during the night, which will help keep you warm. Make sure any rock you shelter under isn't going to fall.

Survival shelters:

There are lots of shelters you can build using mountain debris and a few basic materials. Here are a few basic examples:

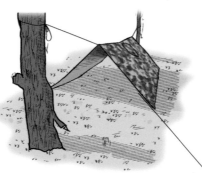

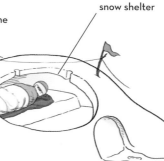

BEAR SAYS

Shelter building takes practice. If you have a go at building different shelters before you travel, you will be better prepared in a survival situation.

poncho A-frame shelter

snow shelter

debris lean-to shelter

MOUNTAIN PLANTS

Mountain plants have to survive in harsh and changeable living conditions. It can be extremely windy, with temperatures that can vary hugely, and the air is very thin and lacking in the carbon dioxide plants need to make food. Soil can be thin, rocky, and lacking in nutrients.

Mountain yucca
This tough evergreen plant can be found in the mountains of Arizona and Mexico. It can be up to 5 m tall, but its trunk is usually less than 30 cm in diameter.

Krummholtz
Krummholtz is German for "twisted wood", and describes the groups of trees in subarctic and subalpine areas that have had their growth stunted and branches shaped by the wind.

Flag tree
This is a type of krummholtz where the branches on just one side have been damaged by the wind.

Fir tree
This is a large evergreen tree often found in mountainous areas. Its wood can be used for building.

Pine tree
These evergreen trees can live for a very long time – sometimes over 1,000 years! Their wood is great for building, and they are often used as Christmas trees. They are common in the Northern Hemisphere.

Korean pine cone
The large seeds (pine nuts) of the Korean pine are edible, and so is the soft, white inner bark. The needles can be steeped in boiling water to make a tea that is high in vitamins A and C.

Alpine flowers
These cope with a short growing season, low temperatures, and dry conditions. In Nepal and India, many families make money from trading in medicinal alpine plants.

ALTITUDE ZONES

- Snow
- Alpine
- Subalpine
- Montane
- Foothill
- Mesomediterranean
- Thermomeso-mediterranean

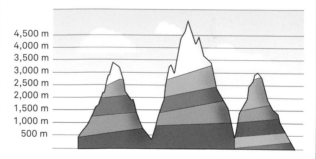

4,500 m
4,000 m
3,500 m
3,000 m
2,500 m
2,000 m
1,500 m
1,000 m
500 m

Altitude zones
Different species of plant and animal live in different parts of a mountain, depending upon the conditions they need to survive. These layers are called altitude zones. You'll notice the vegetation around you change when you reach a new altitude zone.

BEAR SAYS
Captain Cook made his crew drink beer made from spruce trees to stop them getting scurvy during long sea voyages. These plants can also be made into tea.

MOUNTAIN ANIMALS

Animals have a survival advantage over plants because they can move from place to place. Warm-blooded mammals can deal with cold conditions by migrating, hibernating, or seeking shelter. Larger animals tend to migrate, while smaller ones will hibernate.

BEAR SAYS

Goats are extremely useful for meat and milk. They survive well in mountain environments.

Mountain goat
Well adapted to mountain life, goats can easily climb the steepest cliffs thanks to their muscular legs and wide hooves. They eat alpine plants such as fir trees, and can even find food in the snow.

Mount Lyell shrew
This is one of the smallest animals living at high altitude. Because of the amount of energy needed to survive in these conditions, it needs to eat every one to three hours and can eat its own body weight in food in one sitting.

Grizzly bear
Known to scientists as the North American brown bear, this giant hibernates for around six months every year. They can be aggressive to humans, particularly when defending their young. Most of them will avoid humans, and problems usually only occur when they are surprised at very close range.

Condor

The two species of condor are the largest flying land birds in the Western Hemisphere. The California condor can have a wingspan of nearly 3 m. Condors feed on carrion, such as dead seals.

Mountain quail

These birds are easily recognizable by the distinctive feathers on their heads. They live on the ground in the foothills of mountains. They migrate short distances down the mountain by foot in winter.

Mount Graham red squirrel

These tiny squirrels live in a remote mountain range in Arizona. They are diurnal and don't hibernate. They carry out their main activity during the warmest part of the day.

How to survive a bear encounter

- Keep all food packed away – bears have a very strong sense of smell.
- Try to identify the bear.
- Stay calm and quiet. Do not react unless you are sure the bear is charging at you.
- A dog will alert you if a bear is nearby, and the barking may scare the bear away.
- Don't run (they can outrun humans) or hide in a tent (they aren't stupid).
- Play dead (but never for a polar or black bear). Lie flat on your stomach. Spread your legs out and cover the back of your neck with your hands, locking your fingers together. Use your elbows to cover your face. Stay very still and silent. If the bear does manage to roll you over, roll back onto your stomach again, each time.
- Talk in a low voice and wave your arms slowly so the bear knows you are human, not prey.
- A bright, loud bear banger or attack alarm might scare them off.
- If it is dark, shine a torch in their eyes. Their eyesight isn't very good, so this might drive them off.
- Find a way to escape the area, but make sure the bear has an escape route too, otherwise it might feel cornered and lash out.
- Never walk between a mother bear and her cubs.

AVALANCHES

An avalanche is a rapid flow of snow down a slope, growing as it gathers more snow. Rock and debris can also behave the same way, called a rockslide. These can be very dangerous, and even experienced climbers have been badly injured and even killed by falling rocks or snow.

avalanche

BEAR SAYS

Avalanches are most common in the winter and spring when snowfall is heaviest. Be especially careful going up a mountain in these seasons.

What causes an avalanche?

An avalanche can simply be caused by gravity – the sheer weight of the snow is too much for the slope and gives way. Other causes include seismic activity (the Earth's crust moving), change in temperature, rain, skiiers, snowmobiles, and controlled explosive work.

Preventing an avalanche

- If a lot of people are travelling across an area, the snow will become compacted (squashed down) and will be less likely to collapse.
- Experts use explosives to trigger small avalanches to break down unstable areas.
- Snow fences or dams can stop snow building up.
- Planting trees can help to hold snow in place, or at least reduce the flow of the avalanche.

Avalanche equipment

Every member of your group should wear an avalanche transceiver, which can be used to locate them if they get trapped in an avalanche. A collapsible probe can be used alongside a transceiver to find someone who is buried. An ABS backpack contains airbags (like in a car) which can increase the person's volume and keep them close to or on the surface of the snow. It is set off when an avalanche strikes, and needs to be regularly checked.

ABS backpack

How to survive an avalanche

- Take a guide if possible, and make sure you know which areas to avoid.
- Complete an avalanche training course so you can practise what to do.
- Find out about any warning systems in place and follow them.
- Try to escape to the side of an avalanche.
- Hang onto a tree or rock.
- If you are knocked off your feet, set off your ABS backpack and fight for your life.
- Roll to the side or swim upwards.
- Spit out a little bit of saliva as it will run downwards and help you work out which way is up if you are disorientated.
- Before the snow stops moving, cup your hand in front of your face to create an airspace.
- If you are near the surface, try to get an arm or leg out to show others where you are.
- If you can't get out, don't struggle – just enlarge your airspace if necessary.

dig an airspace in front
of your face

ALTITUDE SICKNESS

This medical condition can occur when you travel over 3000 m above sea level. Symptoms begin to show between six and 24 hours after reaching the high altitude, and it can be incredibly dangerous, resulting in serious illness or even death.

Symptoms of altitude sickness

The symptoms of altitude sickness can vary, so it is important to pay attention to your body and, if you start to feel unwell, stop climbing.

headache

tiredness

nausea and vomiting

loss of appetite

dizziness

shortness of breath

Preventing altitude sickness

- Travel slowly to high altitudes — avoid climbing more than 500 m per day.
- Have a rest day every four days.
- Don't fly directly into a high altitude area.
- Take three days to get used to the altitude before going above 3000 m.
- Drink plenty of water.
- Eat a high calorie diet.
- If you start to feel unwell, climb back down to let your body recover.

Treatment for altitude sickness

- Tell others in your group how you feel.
- Stop and rest where you are.
- Don't go any higher for a couple of days after you feel better.
- Treat headaches and sickness with the correct medication, as advised by your doctor.
- Drink lots of water.
- Avoid fizzy drinks, coffee, or anything with caffeine in it.
- If you don't feel better after 24 hours, you should go down to a lower altitude.
- Seek help from a doctor or medical professional.
- There are medications that a responsible adult can bring with them to treat altitude sickness.

BEAR SAYS

When I was preparing to summit Mount Everest, I climbed up and back down multiple times to get my body used to the altitude before I reached the top.

climb slowly –
don't rush

avoid caffeine

get plenty
of sleep

NAVIGATION AND ROUTE FINDING

Mountains aren't just straight up and down, and it's easy to get lost. It is very important that you know how to find your way, and plan out the best and safest route before you go. Always stick to your planned route unless you absolutely have to divert.

Orientation
This is simply working out where you are. You might use a map, compass, or GPS device to help you, or just look out for landmarks.

Navigation
Navigation is working out where you are, where you are trying to go, and choosing and following a route.

Route finding
When you are choosing the right line of travel, you must always take into account your available equipment and the abilities of everyone in your group.

Useful equipment

Compass
There are many types of compass. It is important to choose an appropriate type that you can carry and you know how to use. Compasses always point north, and are best used alongside a map.

Altimeter
A standard altimeter measures air pressure. It can be very precise, but is sensitive to temperature and pressure changes, and will take some practice to use effectively.

GPS
This uses satellites to find a location. It can be used in areas where there are no landmarks, but some parts of the world may not get a satellite signal for the whole day, and it may not work perfectly in extreme cold.

Dead reckoning

This is really just educated guesswork! You can calculate your current position based on where you were before, and the speed and direction of travel. It's best to combine this with other methods as it's very easy to make mistakes using this technique.

thick fog makes it much harder to navigate

Be aware
Objects will look closer than they really are:

- If you look from high ground onto lower ground.
- When looking down a straight, open road.
- When looking over a smooth, uniform surface, like a desert.
- When the light is bright and the sun is shining from behind you.

Objects will look further away than they really are:

- If you look from low ground to higher ground.
- When the object is small in relation to its surroundings.
- When the light is poor, such as dawn or dusk.
- When the object blends into the background.

BEAR SAYS

It's a good idea to take more than one piece of navigation equipment with you in case of any problems.

TRAVELLING ON DIFFERENT TYPES OF TERRAIN

Mountains have all sorts of different terrain, and some are much easier to climb than others. You will need different equipment, clothing, and techniques depending on the type of ground.

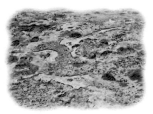

Hard ground
Rest every few steps to allow your leg muscles to recover. Walk uphill in zig-zags rather than straight lines, and avoid crossing your feet when turning corners so you are less likely to fall.

Talus slopes
Step on the uphill side of rocks, and keep checking for any movement underfoot. Avoid walking below other people in case rocks begin to fall.

Scree slopes
Kick in with your toe, make sure you are stable before transferring your weight, and then kick the next step. Scree is extremely tiring to walk on and should be avoided if at all possible.

Snow slopes
Kick steps into soft snow as you go along, so that people behind you can walk in your footprints.

Grassy slopes
Step onto the upper side of any tussocks. This will give you grip and help you to climb. Try to avoid slippery, muddy patches.

Thick brush
Push the brush apart to create a tunnel, or stand on lower branches and hold onto higher branches.

ANCHORS

When you are climbing, you may need to use an anchor. This can be a tree, rock, or a peg hammered into the ground. Anchors are used to hold a rope in place, so that you don't fall when weight is put on the rope.

Tree anchors
A tree is the most obvious natural anchor to use. Check it is well-rooted by pulling and pushing it. Anchor as low as possible to prevent the tree being bent over and keep sap off any equipment.

Rock anchors
Make sure rocks are solid by tapping them and listening to the sound made. Check for loose rocks, as they won't be suitable. Any jagged edges will need to be padded to protect the rope.

Chock stone anchor
A rope can be tied around a rock that has been wedged into a crack. Any chock stone will need carefully testing before it can be used to make sure it is solid enough to take the weight of the person or equipment on the other end of it.

Rock tunnels
Sometimes holes form in rocks, making a tunnel or arch shape. This can be one of the most solid anchor points as the rope can be safely pulled in any direction.

Slings

Slings are very useful, and can be as simple as a loop of webbing, which can be wrapped around your anchor point. There are three ways of attaching a sling to an anchor point.

Drape

This very basic method is when you simply wrap, hang, or drape the sling over or around the anchor point. It still counts as a drape if you have to untie the webbing sling, thread it through, and retie it. It can be used on trees, rock projections, or sturdy rocks, but make sure it's very secure and won't slip.

Wrap

To create a wrap, connect the two ends of your sling together with a carabiner or knot. This is useful on trees or larger rocks, and will provide a little more security than a basic drape as it is less likely to slip.

Girth hitch

A girth hitch is a type of knot that you can use to secure your rope. If you use a girth hitch, the strength of the rope is reduced, meaning you can't lift heavy weights, but it is less likely to slip about.

Artificial anchors

Man-made climbing equipment can be placed into the rock to create an artificial anchor. This can be permanent or removeable – many popular climbing routes may have permanent anchors to help climbers at difficult stretches. Always be careful when relying on artificial anchors and test them properly to make sure they're still sturdy and not damaged.

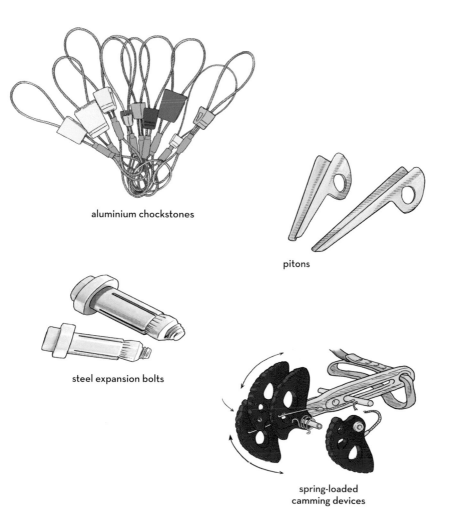

aluminium chockstones

pitons

steel expansion bolts

spring-loaded
camming devices

HILL PEOPLE

Many people live on mountains and hills for a variety of reasons. Mountains have often been regarded as sacred places in some cultures, so it is a privilege to be there. Near the Equator, it is spring all year round so crops can be grown, and in the tropics there is less disease higher up than in the hot lowlands.

Swiss Alps

There are around 14 million people living in the Alps, especially farmers. In the spring, they will move their cattle up to the highest pastures, then come back down in the autumn when the weather gets colder.

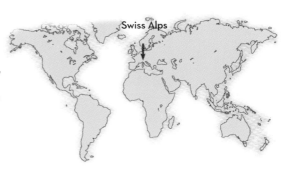

Swiss Alps

kilim

Berber tribe

This group of people live in small communities across North Africa, many in hills and mountains. Often, Berber communities move around rather than living in the same place all year round. Traditionally, Berber men look after livestock while the women look after the family and make things to use at home and to sell, such as beautiful woven carpets called kilims. Music and dancing are very important traditions to Berber people.

Berber tribesperson

Sherpa people

These people live in the Himalaya mountains. Sherpas are regarded as excellent mountaineers and often work as guides for climbers and explorers, including attempts to climb Mount Everest. Tenzing Norgay, one of the first people to climb Everest, was a Sherpa. Because they spend their whole lives at high altitudes, Sherpa people have a much bigger lung capacity than most people, and can survive more easily in the thin air up high mountains.

Gurkhas

Gurkhas were originally Nepalese soldiers who were recruited into the British army. Their name comes from the hill district of Gorkha. They are famous for being incredibly brave and fearless soldiers.

Quechua people

These people, from South America, traditionally farm crops and keep livestock. Their land belongs to the whole community, as opposed to one person. Quechua men and boys wear a distinctive poncho on special occasions. They often wear woolen hats with ear-flaps, and the first one of these that a child receives is knitted by their father.

Chiang Mai hill tribes

Chiang Mai is the largest city in Northern Thailand, and is on the highest mountains in the country. It is a very important part of Thailand – there are over 300 Buddhist temples there. It is possible to visit local hill tribes either on foot or on an elephant, and huge numbers of tourists visit the area every year.

MOUNTAIN SURVIVAL STORIES

While many people enjoy simply walking or taking part in simple climbs in the mountains, there are some people who want to try something nobody else has ever tried before. Every mountain was first climbed by bold explorers like these. Mountaineering is incredibly dangerous, though, and it is important to be well aware of the dangers involved.

Everest 1996

May 1996 saw one of the biggest disasters Mount Everest has ever seen. While several climbers, including guided tour groups, were at high altitude, a huge blizzard hit. Eight people were killed, mostly from exposure to the freezing conditions, or from falls caused by the high winds and low visibility. This disaster raised many questions about whether or not guided tours should be allowed on a mountain as dangerous as Everest.

memorial to people who have died on Everest

Siula Grande 1985

In 1985, two English mountaineers conquered the previously unclimbed West Face of Siula Grande in the Andes. On the way down, though, one man fell and broke his leg. The uninjured man attempted to lower his companion, but they became stuck in a position where they could not see or hear each other. They couldn't move, and the man at the top had to make the difficult choice to cut his friend loose, or stay there and die with him. He cut the rope. Thinking the other man had died, he went down alone. Amazingly, three days later, his friend arrived at their camp... alive! He had crawled five miles through the mountain with a broken leg. This became one of the most incredible survival stories in mountaineering history.

Eiger 1936

Four German and Austrian climbers were
attempting to climb the North Face of the
Eiger, in the Alps, when one of them suffered
a head injury from falling rocks. As they
attempted to abseil back down, three of the
men were killed by an avalanche. Rescuers
were able to get within shouting distance of
the final man, who spent five hours unpicking
the knot in his rope and tying a rescue rope.
Finally, he was able to abseil down, but sadly
died only a few metres from his rescuers.

BEAR SAYS

Even experienced climbers
have been seriously injured or
killed on mountains, so don't
take unnecessary risks. Your
life is more important than
reaching the top.

K2 1953

An American team attempting to climb K2 got caught in a storm near the summit. One of them fell ill, suffering from blood clots which are almost certainly fatal at such a high altitude. At one point during their descent, several of the climbers slipped and fell while roped together. They would certainly have fallen to their death if one very experienced climber hadn't managed to wrap the rope around himself and his ice axe, saving all their lives. The unwell man was killed by an avalanche, but this probably saved the lives of everyone else as they could concentrate on their own survival. Five days later, they reached base camp with frostbite and other injuries – but alive.

Matterhorn 1865

An Englishman and an Italian were competing to be the first to reach the summit of the Matterhorn, which is on the border of Italy and Switzerland. The Englishman and his team got there first, but on the way down one of them slipped and fell, pulling down three other men. Two people clung to the rocks and survived, but the rope broke and the falling men were killed. The survivors were accused of cutting the rope to save themselves, but it was later found out that the rope that broke was old and weak.

Utah 2003

In 2003, a man called Aron Ralston was climbing in Canyonlands National Park, Utah, US. He was climbing in Blue John canyon, a slot canyon, when a 360 kg boulder fell and trapped his right hand against the wall. He couldn't move or break the rock no matter what he tried. On the fourth day of being trapped, he ran out of water and realized that the only way to get out would be to cut off his own arm. He did this using just a pocketknife and survived! He later said that thinking about his family and friends helped him through the ordeal.

BEAR SAYS

If you are climbing, always tell someone where you are going and when you'll be back so they know to send for help if needed.

GLOSSARY

Ascend – to go up

Carrion – dead animals

Census – an official population count or survey

Compacted – squashed together until it is very dense

Descend – to go down

Diurnal – active in the daytime

Dormant – temporarily inactive

Elevation – the height of something, such as a mountain

Evacuate – to leave a dangerous place to get to a safer place

Extinct – no longer in existence

Fault – a gap between tectonic plates in the Earth's crust

Hibernating – a plant or animal spending the winter in a dormant state

Lithosphere – the Earth's crust

Migrating – a creature that moves from one area to another according to the seasons

Polyethylene – the most common type of plastic

Pyroclastics – rocks and other debris thrown into the air by a volcano

Scurvy – a disease caused by a lack of vitamin C

Seismic – to do with earthquakes

Slot canyon – a deep, narrow canyon

Subalpine – the mountain zone just below the treeline

Subarctic – areas just below the Arctic Circle

Tectonic plate – a segment of the Earth's crust that can move.

Terrain – a certain type of land

Turpentine – a smelly oil used to clean paint brushes

Vegetation – the plants found in a particular habitat